A BIG Thank You for a Wonderful Year.

with love from:

WORKPLACE WONDERS

This notebook belongs to

Printed in Great Britain
by Amazon

63231399R00066